THE MECHANICAL BIRD

The Mechanical Bird

Asa Boxer

SIGNAL EDITIONS IS AN IMPRINT OF VÉHICULE PRESS

Published with the generous assistance of The Canada Council for the
Arts, the Book Publishing Industry Development Program of the
Department of Canadian Heritage, and the Société de développement des
entreprises culturelles du Québec (SODEC).

SIGNAL EDITIONS EDITOR: CARMINE STARNINO

Cover design: David Drummond
Photo of author: Jennifer Varkonyi
Set in Minion by Simon Garamond
Printed by Marquis Book Printing Inc.

LIBRARY AND ARCHIVES CANADA CATALOGUING IN PUBLICATION DATA

Boxer, Asa
The Mechanical Bird / Asa Boxer
Poems.
ISBN 978-1-55065-222-7
I. Title.

PS8603.097868G69 2006   C811'.6   C2007-90444-3

Published by Véhicule Press, Montréal, Québec, Canada
www.vehiculepress.com

Distribution in Canada by LitDistCo
orders@litdistco.ca

Distributed in the U.S. by Independent Publishers Group
www.ipgbook.com

Printed in Canada

This book is dedicated to the memory of my father,
Avi Boxer

Acknowledgements

These poems were published, often in different versions, in *The New Canon: An Anthology of Canadian Poetry* (Véhicule, 2005), *Montréal vue par ses poètes* (an anthology of Montreal poets – Memoire D'encrier 2006), *Poetry London*, and *EnRoute*. "Maledicta," "The Gear Train," and "Spell for a Wardrobe" were first published on-line by *Nthposition*.

"To Needle the Earth" was selected for inclusion in the Oxford Poetry Broadside series. Poems from the third section were previously published by Montreal Books Press in a chapbook called *Lies*. And an early version of the last section, entitled "The Workshop," was awarded first prize in the 2004 CBC/*EnRoute* poetry competition.

What you hold in your hand is the product of a community of very talented, very meddlesome people. Thanks to my mother, Sarah Engelhard, Michael Harris, Ricardo Sternberg, David Antoine Williams, David Solway, Eric Ormsby, Leonard Cohen, Geoffrey Rayburn, and Amanda Cockburn who said, "Write me a poem about a polar bear." Thanks to all at Véhicule, especially to Simon Dardick and Carmine Starnino. And fiduciary thanks are owed to the Canada Council for the Arts for a generous grant that loosened my financial fetters enough to complete this project.

Contents

THE MAP

puts the bird's eye in the hand of the traveller.
His difficulty is that a bird's vision is one-eyed,
gut-headed, and cocked on the rudest of schemes.

The near-reptilian point of view, the focus on food,
on the routes of entry and escape would be an aid,
if the traveller could tell the downtown from the uptown.

Every which way he turns it, though, the map becomes
a different animal. A butterfly, it folds its paper
wings; it is the world pinned in place and laid flat.

A moment later, it's a magic carpet to Baghdad,
then a Chinese folding screen, next, an accordion.
Each turn and fold makes an origami creature of the world.

The traveller lays the map aside. He wants to find
what's off the chart. He seeks the obscure haunts,
the overlooked alleys, the flutterings of life not catalogued.

Butterfly and moth see the world in spirals.
They fly like leaves caught in a whirlwind.
The traveller pursues the eccentricities of their movement.

He wishes to make of himself a stranger,
to follow alien customs, to learn a new language,
its rhythms and inflections, its sharps and its flats

along the curve of an arc, that, like their dancing,
is as peculiar as a moth's. He believes that by retraining
his eye to see, by learning a new etiquette for welcoming

and bidding farewell, by overwriting excitement
with another vocabulary for the upsurge of joy
or hatred; he will gain a hawk's eye of insight,

develop a migratory instinct, understand the globe
and its myriad of signs. The map impressed upon him
to the deepest vein, he'll move with the world under his skin.

THE TRAVELLER

The traveller's wish is to touch the vanishing point,
to arrive at the crux, to stand in the deepest place,
the narrows where the elements, upon parallel lines,
finally converge. He seeks the poles and peaks.

He knows that the ground and immediate air
where a rainbow comes to rest is a place where you stand
without knowing it. A traveller knows that the true gold
is the hope that comes with the digging,

that striking gold is the end of the road and time to rest.
Time for learning charm and tasting wine; time for building cities,
aeroplanes, for dreaming up pleasures and palaces larger than life.
But the traveller's instinct makes of munificence a trifle,

treats it like a delicate inflorescence of forget-me-nots
in a roadside ditch. To the traveller, a great war is run of the mill:
a mass slaughter of chickens for a stew of hearts.
He trusts the litter that catches in the autumn rake;

it puts on no airs. He trusts the crab-apple and the way it rots.
To the traveller, understanding is a brief state
of mental arrest. It gels at the twinkling between water
and ice. Feeling lost, he looks up at the flickering stars.

He knows it all in a gulp, ages condensed into a twitch of space.
He must close his eyes to understand. He must rest and recover.
He must mine all his stories. He must grub up a life,
every root within him dreaming up love.

THE POLAR BEAR

At the polynia, the polar bear mills like a vacationer
around a pool, only this bear's pleasure is wrapped in stillness,
a sub-zero oasis in baffles of snow. Lumbering, he
travels his seasons driven by hunger, moults in the spring,

winters in the den he dug with the wide paw
now thrown over his snout to keep warm. The bear
like a blanket of snow, recovering. His muscles
like a grenade, a land-mine, a trap-door.

His jaw like a fox-trap, a clamp. His paws,
their non-retractable claws, his forty-two teeth, dead still
as a hunter, like a bullet asleep in its chamber.
His organs are slow-burning embers, his brain, a tank of gasoline.

The bear dreams of a berry on the tip of a twig,
the weight of a seal swollen like a fruit on the claw of a branch.
His swaddle of blubber twitches at the imagined windfall,
the thump of a fist of raw flesh pounding at his icy door.

In his sleep, he's turning seal into bear.
The polar bear is an animal of ice who must rest
or swim for the heat that consumes him. His fur
is a white fire, blazing from his charred-black skin.

CAT NAP

Enjoying rest, the house-cat wears her twilight coat, curls up,
and disappears among the waves of a rumpled blanket. So softly
      does she sleep,
it seems birds could fold safely into her paws, mice slip out of her
      pockets.
But in her brain, the owl flicks awake the dim lanterns of its eyes.

The mice stash their tiny beds safely under the boards of the
      hardwood floors.
The birds have worried in the eaves, tucking in their quiet nests,
      weaving whirlwinds
of twigs, pine needles, and string from the forest's busy kitchen,
      where the fall
is cooking up a dreadful storm; mixing in every wild spice the
      forest can afford.

The woodpecker has peppered the trees and peppered the air with
      its knocking.
By ant-back, bee-sock, and squirrel-cheek, the forest is getting
      carried away.
The forest is shedding and shifting while the cat twitches an ear,
      listening
as the porcupine munches the main beam of the house down to
      the sweet core.

When the main beam snaps and the house leans with a groan of
      steel and wood;
when its hidden shelters crack and betray the mice at their
      gnawing; the eyelids
of the cat will split, her eyes break open, her claws slip out. She'll
      leap at the bird,
toy with the mouse, and hunt till the buzz of the forest is caught.

THE TURTLE AND THE STONE

The turtle moves as slowly as he does,
because he desires to be counted
among the stone-cold, the rock-solid.

The turtle moves as carefully as he does,
because he wants to live forever
and somewhere in his amphibious brain,

the longevity of coral, the persistence
of mountains and boulders have impressed
him with their stubborn immobility.

The turtle is but a step away from stone,
and he hopes, each day, to slow his pace,
to approach, within a fraction, a dead halt,

and thus come so near death as to learn
the secrets of eternity, and strike the deal
struck by stone.

THE DAMSELFLY

She is a surveyor of the lakefront, the forest, and the field.
Shifting from angle to angle, the damselfly stops at intervals
to triangulate the picture. She dead-halts in air, threadbare
wings moving so fast, they disappear and leave her dangling,

perfectly still, a hovering stick, a broken rule. She darts
and ducks the deadly possibilities. Her survival depends
upon her ability to distinguish between lizard and rock.
She can't afford to confuse the quality of patience

with the unshakeable promise of stone. The lizards
attract her with the humility of their devotions, imitating
the hard modesty of pebble and rock. From their head-bones
to their tails, they offer the safe shelter of a jagged ridge.

But theirs is the cold hunger of stone. In her world,
even the rocks hide deadly tongues. This is why
the damselfly darts and flits and buzzes in fits.
She too grows stiff as stone, ever on edge,

anticipating a sudden softening of the hard world,
expecting an agile pounce, awaiting a limber lunge.
She only settles because she must. She's wired stiff
on a turtle's back, her thousand eyes alert but unaware

that an eyeball—slow as the world's turning—
has peeled back its green lid, that a wrinkled head
has decided to inch toward water. The mountains
and the rooted trees are about to topple, the anchored

lake, about to spill its awful weight. She hovers in place
as the turtle-shell leaves her feet with a gulp. She is elated.
She is the measure that flies in the face of nature. Now,
as the damselfly passes, every stone holds its tongue.

THE SNAKE AND THE LAMB

The snake opened up like a tunnel to the womb.
The lamb slid in. The snake clamped down.
And now the snake seems pregnant with the lamb.
And now the lamb sleeps in the skin of a snake.

At first he felt a tickle by his hind-leg, then a brush
past his shank, a caress across the chest, a nudge
past the ears like a mothering tongue. Then a squeeze
growing tighter, like the love of ten-thousand wombs.

Though the lamb kicked for air, the snake held fast,
for the love of a snake holds tighter than life.
The world went black. The lamb fell limp.
The snake then bound and bagged his prey.

And now, the reptile troubles over each woolly bite;
he must stomach every ingredient of lamb,
the tough and the tender, the flesh and the fat.
Every last cell of snake must come to the table.

Every last scale must welcome the lamb.
In their dreams they are one where awake they struggled.
The lamb must sleep to quiet the snake.
The snake must sleep to swallow the lamb.

MALEDICTA

A pest on the fox for slaughtering hens. May the pepper gun's blast
be at her tail, may the kernels set in her skin. May her fur catch fire
and burn without end. Let her blaze through the forest. Let her trail
be known; let the dead wood catch and glow with the foxfire.

An affliction on the rat for polluting the collective grain.
Let her fur grow in tufts. Let her skin be a scab over a sack of decay.
Let her tail seem a rigid worm. May she bed with the maggot.
Let the biting flea keep her twitching, a restless nest of disease.

A hex on the crow for taxing the corn. Let his call rasp
through his beak; may he never learn to sing. Let his feathers
be pitch. May the sight of him be a harbinger of death.
Let the crow be ever at assembly, defending his uneasy perch.

Torment the lovers for raiding the coop, pilfering the eggs,
and sucking them dry. May their appetites increase.
May they grow fat behind a picket fence.
May they have more children than love can afford.

An apocalypse on the conquering army that spilled salt
on the bountiful land. May the earth parch where they settle.
May the local creatures die in hordes. Let the generals
and captains be witness to the surrender of the living world.

A pox upon the planet for its tsunamis and its droughts.
Let the moon pull at the sheets of ocean and the earth
forever turn in its sleep. Let a curse of creatures blast
its mountains, drill its crust, and drink its sweetest waters.

Blast the cosmos for gripping the planet with tongs of ice,
for holding it up to the sun, for keeping the world boiling
at the core, for troubling its surface with disastrous quakes.
May an efficient race disfigure space and dust away the moon.

TERROR IN JERUSALEM

Terror lives in the cornerstones, and in the small
monuments around what seems like every bend.
Terror at the children murdered in their dawdling.

A small, cold slab of stone marks the morbid place
where young muscles squirmed a pace
like worms against the dust; and then,
like worms, fell flaccid and gave up.

A candle flickers by the stone; its heat throbs
like the heart that beat the blood to earth.
And the flame that tugs and flashes
on the wick, flashes and tugs on the collective brain.

These children are the grim cement of a nation,
the crumbling stonework, the shaky foundation.
Their bones are the hardware underlying the infrastructure;
they are the fodder, fuelling the slogans and campaigns.

The valley of Gehenna is fertile;
centuries of infant sacrifices, and it burns green.
Now, the surrounding desert is thirsty.
And not an Abraham hesitates over his Isaac;

not a soul feels the angel's restraining hand.
Instead, the radio keeps a finger on the pulse,
and we listen for its announcements and commands.

AMAD

Amad has the look of a star.
He should be flickering across a movie screen,
singing the way he sings over the dishes,
only singing over pretty women, dancing for the world.

But on Amad's planet, the stars sing far away
or not at all. His village will not see a star
in any other way. The stars, they say,
must know and keep their places till the end of days.

Amad is a fixed star; fixed above a dirty sink.
He doesn't feel hallowed or august; he feels
his fingers shrivelling, senses something vaguely elliptical
in the movement of his labours. Amad is dependable.

He wouldn't murder. He's docile and works as he must,
in summertime construction for a paunchy slave-driver.
Face it. He's not an actor, because he can't read a script.
He's a horse, an ox, a mule. He pulls cement.

He must keep his wife in jewellery; and she'll take
nothing but gold. He mustn't seek pleasure in drink.
And no escape in hashish. 'My village,' he explains.
Amad is nineteen years old. He wants a girlfriend.

And I wonder where. Where in hell, between now
and his curfew? Where between the impatient
soldiers at the border? Between ID checks,
permits, papers, questions, sirens, murder?

Where between wife and homestead?
Where in this godforsaken desert?
An earthquake could hardly disquiet deeper.
Where, in God's name, will Amad find love?

IN HITLER'S HOLY LAND

In Hitler's Holy Land, the Jews all live in fear.
Hitler drives the Hebe still; and still he goads you like sheep.
He shapes your political bleating, your woolly sense of nationhood.

Hitler is the unnamed father of the Holy Land,
the profoundly silent guest at every Independence Day.
He gave you, kikes, victims to count and tales of survival to recount.

Either Hitler gave what God withheld, or Hitler
played the holy crook and prod to ghettoise an ancient strip
with all you varied breeds of Yid… and Abra-cadaver, Allah Kassam…

the most efficient death camp ever found. O, Hitler tied a black,
ironic ribbon round his gift; Hitler tied an impossible bow:
to disentangle its furious knot, you must cut at the eye of its bloom.

You must give your golden teeth and clip your nails and shear
your hair and keep your gaze upon the ground while suicides blow
their deadly flowers everywhere, and your children pick bones.

VICTIMS

We are collecting our victims.
We are cataloguing them alphabetically in books,
engraving them into glistening cenotaphs.
We sing songs. Our histories trouble over them.

The army rewards its victims with rank,
and makes of death a stripe, a bar, a star,
a step up in the world. But why lay power
upon a dead man's shoulders?

O, it's a desperate tribe, that dies by the busload.
We are collecting our victims. We house them
like gods, in elaborate shrines. The tourists pass through
with their guides. All victims are perfect,

all of them shine. The arts adore and adorn them.
A victim is saintly and serene.
A victim is meek and begs only one thing;
that you dutifully kill for its cause.

TO NEEDLE THE EARTH

Its blossoms growing blind with anticipation, the tree
that's been training, tying knots in its skin,
and from them flying a thousand little flags and kites
holds its sway over the ground. Nest-worthy and cradle-

sure, a hand to the bird, a loom to the spider, a toe-
hold to the lichen, a back-scratch to the bear,
a spiralling argument to the chipmunk and squirrel,
a wild and airborne botanical town. Whatever its lean,

in hush and in howl, the tree holds its poise.
To every claw-slash and talon-bite, the wood
responds with sweetness; but the sap that seals the score
and suckles a thousand stems will capture and kill a fly.

Before it unfurls forms more outrageous than a fine-
toothed green, the tree must channel a sapling's enthusiasm
to twig, must run with the amber it finds in the rot, blossoms
stirred up from the syrup-song of its bark-lodged heart.

Berries swell and stop the flowers; gone is the flare,
and gone are the delicate powders. Nutshell, pinecone,
calabash and pith; the tree hatches its palate-baffling fruit,
and seeds to needle the earth to its works.

THE LOBSTER

Sunk behind its dingy window
in a supermarket aquarium,
the lobster turns a muzzy eye
on the great *élan* of air.

Exposed to every scrutiny; it waits,
claws bound, an antenna snapped.
Not a crawl-space, nor a shadow,
still as stone; invisible, it hopes.

It hopes a lobster's coral hopes,
cramped upon a shallow shelf.
But its brains cannot conceive the sea
outside the lobster-shell. Desire, thus,

keeps slim to fit the narrow life within.
You will never hear the baffled lobster cry,
"What crime could be so great it moved the sea
to single-out a bloated shrimp like *me*?"

It's a muffled clatter, this life that smudges by:
rattling cartloads of death perambulate past;
smutchy children nose and thump the glass;
vague eyes and teeth wink pearl hints

of what's to come. This wispy world
suffused with light; a lobster's carnival-
afterlife. Where each impression colours and brews
through nerve, and muscle, and sinew.

Where a thorny heat keeps life fired
to a reddening shriek. And God,
God boils it through.

MACRO-ECONOMICS

We flatten to slip into currency, to be rung up and rung out
and registered with the sigh and the click of a sliding drawer.

From pocket to till, our souls rub away,
or dispense another nano-ounce of heat in transit by wire.

A last electronic blip zaps a filament more of our power
into stark black codes for another burial by file.

These migratory transactions take no commercial breaks.
Ruthless, they take stock and transfer terms without notice.

The dead have turned to bread in the beaks of a million birds.
Yes. And on the windshields of a million cars,

the dead find ways to make of themselves a casual reminder
of the wicked surprises that may whistle downwind to shock you.

With all the bare wire wiring our closest friends,
how does one grasp and not deal in pain?

If I have hurt, it was a bovine dullness that drove me,
a too-rough pursuit of the colour in a shaken cloth.

But don't forgive a bull on the grounds of his charge.
Forgiveness is dissipation.

Like a potentate, let only scraps fall
to the cats that plead most convincingly.

And inhale the uric and fecal consequences; the outcomes
of what falls from a careless jaw and a hasty hand.

I hesitate at the trigger of a .22 to count my bullets;
there will never be enough to clean up this garden.

One round. Two. And the ravens heave away carrion.
The rest I leave to the sun.

TWO STITCHES

My cousin was speaking of his toe,
the one the lawnmower severed
one sweltering summer afternoon.

"Two stitches," he explained.
"Just two stitches for the big toe."
So he asked, "Why so stingy
on the thread? Had I known
I'd've brought my own."

Two stitches do the trick.
One above and one below.
The skin, the nerve, the bone
must make their ways alone.
Too many stitches just make a mess.
Two stitches do the trick.

Like lovers, I suppose.
For all the deft needling,
the practiced fingers,
the tender kisses, each kiss a stitch,
two stitches would do the trick.

And if we were torn from each other,
quite suddenly, as if by a lawnmower,
one quietly humming afternoon
sometime in June…
If this were to happen, what would we do?

What kind doctor with an understanding
of stitches would be able to get past
all the well-needled stitching and find
the two delicate places, and say, "Here.
Here."—just like that?

THE BIRCHBARK CANOE

Shape me a paddle for this birchbark canoe.
The river is moving with the old and the new,
for the cold cannot freeze its deeps
though it locks it down in ice
and renders unusable the birchbark canoe.

Make the boat ready when the river is free
and the ground thaws through.
Inuit, Micmac, and Woodland Cree.
When the weather is ready, they will all
pile into the birchbark canoe.

Come with your legends of beaver and bear.
Throw in the armies of Wolfe
and Montcalm. Then let their swords fall
to the hands of Suzanne by the river to rust.
Hold the boat steady for our hero, Louis Cyr,

stronger than horses, five feet of mountain.
We will carve our totems
like the river carves its banks,
whittle our brushes from reed-beds,
pluck our pens from the snow-owl's wing,

set our stroke to the sway of the river
that never stops moving with the old and the new.
While we wait for the ice to break,
for the paddle to be hewn, we will dine
with Karavis, toast the Syrian al-Maghut,

make space for Robbie Burns,
Duddy K. can come too.

Our canoe is getting crowded, but never fear:
Louis Cyr will manage our impossible portage
and Kravitz will buy us the land.

If we need a decent legend, Karavis
will bring his to the waiting canoe.
And if we lose our sense of outrage
at the slaughter in this new world
we'll prick our ears when al-Maghut sings

the songs of the knife and grenade.
Hostie. Chalice. Tabernacle. All adrift
in the Saint Lawrence River, our words
drown each other, competing to stay afloat.
No bother, Burns will pen joual,

and Garneau deliver franglais.
The season of the sonnet is here;
the bongos play under the wings of freedom,
at the foot of the hill. And Nelligan,
his crystal nerves melting like icicles,

enough to raise the river an inch or two,
will carry us through the fertile muck,
under the birds on the wire. Though we're lodged
like a rock in the throat of a cockatoo,
as the river keeps moving through the old and the new,

our legends will carry us through.

FASHION STATEMENTS

Combat boots lives in a walking entanglement,
A muscular garden of tattoos in a tank-top,
Eats gold-fish for breakfast.
Nobody fucks with combat boots,
Not even tank-top,
And since she lives in this garden,
No one dares fuck with tank-top either.

Tie sits at another table, knotted and coifed
After-shave wafting like an olfactory ad
As if freshly torn from a glossy page.
His jacket has many hidden closets and rooms
He keeps various parts of his identity there.
Tie has just turned platinum.
He keeps this fact tucked in a room close to his heart.
When tie reaches in there,

Cell-phone lights up. Cell-phone loves tie.
In fact, she just dies for tie. She gave him the watch;
He gave her the chain around her neck.
He wears black, she, white;
They are ready to be planted in a wedding cake.

Jeans has a petite tattoo:
On her thigh, a butterfly.
Above this a garden, further still some hills for it to play in.
Her mind is full of poems.
Jeans wears glasses
Cut her face abstract. Jeans keeps a tight bun,
And makes love to many a one like cords.

Cords keeps a tight face, a toilet-seat face.
This is because he thinks.
Jeans too is scrunchy in the face.
Both faces are a collection of features inching toward each other
asymptotically toward some inscrutable point.
Cords writes poems; jeans loves every line.
One can barely keep her hands off the other
As they sit here at the café, smoking lustily
Eyes alight with innuendo.

And then there is you and me.
You, of course, are perfect, my dear.
We are the salt among this peppering,
Naked and marked by nothing but birth.
No odours but those of our respective organisms.
But, my love, I am afraid that we are being stared at.
And tie is looking rather offended.
Combat boots is squinting at you,
And jeans, I think, wants a piece of you too.
Cell-phone is checking us out in the mirror of her compact.
Cords looks constipated with thought.
And here comes the waitress with our order.

WHEN I WAS WATER AND YOU WERE A TREE

In truth your breasts were the blinders
that came with the bridle you buckled to me.
I was in your arms for the whole nine yards,
my nose in your cleavage and I couldn't see—
till my eyelids cupped my eyes in a dream
in which I was water and you were a tree.

But I was not water enough to get in your hair
and be wrung into beads on your breast,
and you were not tree enough to stay in one place,
or if you were a tree, your flowers were swelling
with fruit that no tree ever grew; and too quickly
for one pair of hands to know what to do.

SPELL FOR A WARDROBE

Each pocket, let him in. Each stitch, hold to him.
Each earring, listen. Bracelets, go; belts, loosen;
broaches, pierce; buttons, pop to point the way.

This golden necklace-clasp I clasp to me
will show its eye to sign he thinks of me,
and rest upon my breast in sympathy.

Each quarter-inch this cinching garter slip,
each rung that tracks along each stocking's run
tell the mounting minutes that his mind's on me.

This hairpin came with wishes from his heart.
If it slip, he's been untrue; a poisoned pin
he pinned to you. Return it to his heart.

Wardrobe, wardrobe, hold me in foretelling
folds. Sparkle and crinkle, and, swish, it's told.

A WOBBLY TABLE

One tilt, you slip, and slice your finger-tip.
A table that totters is blackest of luck.
A teetering table can move on its own
and summon the poltergeist into your house.

A rickety table'll hex a home's toil,
spill milk, shed blood, tax ale, leak oil.
An unsteady table spells divorce in the number
of years there are feet between table and floor.

Eat at a wobbly table, all your fruits,
even those dangling from the tended fruit trees,
are bound to bruise and blindly turn to rot.
And all your progeny come to naught.

Where a little salt spills, a little life is lost.
An unstable table topples a home.

THE MECHANICAL BIRD

being uncounted among nature's holdings
in God's Domesday Book, is more exotic
than toucan, ostrich, peacock, and flamingo.

She engages the heart with the pathetic,
unintuitively geared arc of her flight
until her spring winds down with a crank.

And she engages the heart
in her suit of dead feathers,
and with the worn, yellow glass of her eyes.

Not in lock, nor stock, nor barrel
during the time of census;
forgotten during God's dispensation of grace;

and overlooked during the allotment of will.
All the more alluring, her awkwardness,
the novelty and the humour of her ugliness.

Her eye unlit by hunger,
her neck without a strut
to swing to. There is a key to wind

her wings, but none to lighten her gait;
yet see how she folds, perches,
and warbles with the rest.

THE MECHANICO-CORPUSCULAR AGE

They threw a fine net over the planet, squeezed it for co-ordinates.
Every point became a joint, a corner, a significant meeting place.
Finding latitude was easy: read the polestar's pitch; longitude,
however, was like a lane passed blindly in a blizzard.

The earth, you see, in its slow, confusing spin, unscrolls
the stars across its southern screen like snow, a very, very slow
snow, a confounding pageant of brilliance in motion
that takes us all in till we lose track of time,

there being no still point: no cynosure
anywhere along the arc of east and west.
And part of the problem was the moon.
They knew it had menstrual phases,

but these were predictable; it was its refusal
to behave like clockwork: its light way with gravity;
its attractions, repulsions; its triangular interplay
with sun and sea; the storms that make it impossible

to determine if it is where you want it to be
at the time you expected it would be there,
that unreliable, luminous flake of a moon.
Home-time was needed to compare with time on the go;

the difference between them, converted to distance,
would keep you on course, and save you from thirst,
from boredom, from wreckage, from scurvy or worse.
But the moon, being bad with appointments,

was no better than a good dead-reckoning,
a weather forecast, a prayerful guess.
A decorous moon would have made the sky a perfect clock,
but this moon dawdled, its head in the clouds.

So they engineered a mechanical clock,
a well-behaved universe in a nutshell, clean cut,
bejewelled teeth, and a steady, sickling hand.
Ingenuity set tribal toil ticking toward a bang.

Not some dirty freak of a faceless multiverse
with unpredictable twitches and ticks; it was
something smooth, calculating, steady-pulsed, shiny;
this minute machine divided the globe and co-ordinated war.

THE GEAR TRAIN

The pallet kisses the scape wheel, kisses the pallet.
The gear train is moved by the number of their kisses.
The gear train, a clock's brain, translates this touch,

this physical impulse into figure and fact;
it makes of inner love a discipline of hands,
clocking how long love will last

through these endless enumerations: there are
infinite ways to read the contours of its face,
there are seven hundred ways to call its name.

The train dotes on itself, an instrument of worry;
it dispenses anxiety over every missed beat, every missed call,
perhaps transmits its own flaws and hang-ups

to the turns and the swings of its clockwork heart.
A lady's hair and a kiss of dust can upset the whole machine.
Friction in the train can leave the pendulum plumb dead.

The gear train doesn't tick or beat; it grinds its steel teeth.
It mills the minutes out of hours, the seconds
out of minutes, drops the hour like a husk.

WHEN THE SCAPE WHEEL BREAKS THE VERGE

Six hundred sixty teeth will crash down,
the clattering gears come loose from their train
when the scape wheel breaks the verge.

The force driving time will spin away
with a mad buzz, a whir of relief
from the spring coiled up in its drum.

The people'll be freed of the bands
on their wrists; and the magnates,
from the chains to their pockets.

The first sign will be dead silence:
nothing rhythmic, nothing sounding
like a kiss; not a cricket, not a tick.

When the scape wheel breaks the verge,
there'll be panic. There'll be no clock
to fix the time and place of death.

And no hour will reckon when to fight
and when make up; when to sleep
and when wake up. And not a prayer,

not a poem, not a foot of verse
to count on.

DEAD-RECKONING

Pitch an empty barrel ahead of the plashing bow.
Tell the speed of its trail astern in beads
on a rosary, holding count of Ave Marias.

Hope up the sea's guarded, secret longitudes
by counting blessings, living uncertainly
with busy angels, even busier devils, miracles.

If your ship's travelling at three
and a quarter Ave Marias, if you're
travelling at the speed of verse;

you're liable to end up anywhere,
you may even end up cursed, so go ahead,
add an extra Ave Maria for safe measure,

overestimate the speed; expect land early and look
ahead to the clouds for refracted tinges of algae.
An experienced mariner steers clear of verse,

pitches a log-and-knotted-line over the waking stern,
gives the minute-glass a turn, then counts the knots
logged out to sea in the time it takes a thousand grains

of sand to trickle down. Even then, with poor maps,
phantom islands creeping from the burning mists were known
to attack like sudden dragons and snap a solid hull to timber,

until a steady clock was built to do away with dragons.
It ruled the world, governed direction, dispensed security.
It sharpened our sense of imminence: it reinvented love.

HOW TO LIE

Keep it simple, tidy,
take a noncommittal stance.
Most of all be flip
and keep it uncontrived.

Contrivedness is avoided
by steering clear of rhyme;
nothing so neat as to catch
like a barb in the mind. So memory

must rely on subtler work-a-day
schemes, the way you keep your PIN,
the access code to your e-mail,
the combination to your lock.

Pitch your lie on a chunk or two
of the bedrock of figure and fact
and remember that the greatest lies
are delivered with a smile.

A good liar knows it's a bad rap
to be right once too often.
A good liar lets you win a time or two,
and every few or so he hustles you.

A liar is a gregarious creature,
he makes many friends and quick:
talks of their enemies with enmity;
talks of their friends amicably. Frequently agrees.

In company of enemies, then,
act the spy on the friends you told
you'd spy for until the camps
of us and them are entirely scrambled.

Surely, this is the liar's gift:
to find at last a lunar gravity,
a mind that won't pursue
effects to causes, nor rig up pasts

to chain to the present moment—
because the diligent liar
knows his lying well enough
to know himself in truth.

HOW TO GET AWAY WITH A LIE

For godsakes, do not tilt
your chin sheepishly down;
the beans could spill
with any wobble in your composure.

Butter your words on both sides,
not thickly, but with finesse.
Keep your fingers a little greasy too.
The trick's to give reality the slip,

to find a way to squeeze by.
A well-told lie furtively drops a banana peel,
and drops a few performance enhancers, too,
to buy a few seconds' time in the race against truth.

Drop your lie with a creased forehead, and a whistle,
eyes rolled up to the suddenly interesting sky.
Like the bargain hunter, the lover, and the cat,
a lie should prowl with disinterested eyes.

The trick's to set up near a well-trafficked place,
a web of your own composing, to catch,
wrap up the facts in neat bundles, and juice them dry.
A good liar must be arachnid, then; he must run with eight legs.

When all precautions fail, and a curious finger
picks at the suspension ropes, and your network shivers
an ominous morse into your toes,
lift your hairy ass-of-a-body, scurry off;

and for godsakes, don't get cornered:
the idea's to get the sense of verity to defect
from another's neural network to your own
without getting nailed like a witless fly.

Cross your heart and hope to die,
swear on any grave or relic they dig up;
bring along some brand of proof,
then treat the lie as you would treat the truth.

HOW TO CATCH A LIE

Tricky: A rod and net
and a good pair of gloves
won't cut it.

Even if the line
is hundred-pound test
and invisible,

even if the gloves
hold their own, it's unwise
to fish the solitary lie

where it schools;
you're liable
to be drawn overboard

with fishy philosophies,
like the squamous fascisti,
liable to be capsized

by a gam of tall tales,
to be hounded by
the notorious pack of lies,

then cleverly sidetracked
by a skulk of red herrings
into a wild goose chase.

You're bound, in short,
to find your lie
along with all its inquisitions,

when all you have to do
is torture truth.
One is advised, therefore,

against the hunting down
of lies, even if you hunt them
gently with a net.

A lie's more subtle
than your average butterfly,
and the ones you catch,

up close and past
the paints and powders,
are wormier lies

than you can fathom.
Even the weathered chaser of lies
runs the terrible risk

of arresting truth
for suspicion of lying.
Of all the things to catch,

the truth's the worst,
with its mouthful of bones,
its eviscerating stare.

Oh, the truth is raw
as a case of herpes.
Nerveless. Blistering. Contagious.

But if you insist on hunting lies,
familiarise yourself with
their habits and haunts.

You'll catch them, for instance,
in the groins of lovers, you'll pull
them like threads from your sleeve.

You'll catch their hands
in sugar bowls and cookie jars,
or picking through your pockets.

You'll catch them neatly
catalogued in the library.
You'll catch them by one ear

eavesdropping on your talk,
the picture of dreamy innocence,
as if planets away behind you

in the line-up for the bank-machine.
As a hunter of lies, you'll know
you're on their radar, they're plotting,

that you must be swift,
for they'll have soon spied out
the ethical key to your mind,

so that when you are condemned
to negotiate that single lie's release,
you'll have mobilised a thousand lies,

and contracted mercenary lies
to contain what your crumbling heart
now realises was one very

slippery fish of a lie.

SOLVING A LIE

The sky clouded over, turned a light-polluted red,
and a hackle-raising wail rose from the broken heart
of a crazed adolescent dumped into the night.

She cried a holler from her curled toes
and from the fists of stone beneath her toes.
And with all the mighty earth beneath the stone

surging like a power in her bare legs;
she wailed like death for the whole
stinking neighbourhood

to hear and to wake
with a hatchet in its dreams,
because the world had to know.

This was, it must be said,
the worst breakup
in the History of Breakups,

a history, I might add,
that I found thereafter
in seven books on the subject:

two recorded by a Roman poet
a third one by an English clerk,
a fourth by an English entertainer,

the fifth, by German brothers,
one, in Arabic, about a king
who wedded and beheaded women,

before his daily brunch was served,
until Sheherezad, who liked to talk,
interwove a thousand tales like a tapestry

to involve the deadly ear in sleep,
and tease his brutal mind to imagery,
and wake and trick his rotten reason,

and delay his sense of night and day
by lying in a captivating way,
and with all her mental might.

The seventh book, in Hebrew,
raises every dirty breakup in antiquity,
even milk serves murder in that black book.

This was all I found,
nothing academic,
only spurious reports

of a long and hurtful history
anchored in the genetic roots
that run the human race.

I deduced, however (returning
to the lady's claim)
that the worst breakup in history

would have to be worse than
a black eye, and worse still
than waking with her hair cut off;

worse than being starved
in a cold, dank spire, worse;
worse than being ravaged,

and worse than afterward
having her tongue cut out,
her head lopped off, far worse

than having her own children
slaughtered and served to her for dinner,
worse indeed than after dinner finding out,

oh worse, far, far more immediate than all that.
And I know just what she meant.

GREASE AND RUST

Every tool is the anointed king of its work:
even as it waits and fades into the general mess,
even if it sinks to the status of a handle
poking from a box behind the curtain

beneath the counter, a wire coiled
round the grip, its head near drowned
in a pool of screws. A coat of oil
repels corruption while the handle waits.

The vise is seasoned black with grease.
Black grease is cleanest in the shop
where rust is the enemy; clean means
strongholds of metal free of rust.

Everything blessed with oil, like the hair
of heroes and saints, prophets and messiahs.
Grease fills the surface-scratch that'll never heal,
settles deep into the score against all agents of rust.

Each tool is patient and confident it is meant
for the job it was designed to do best; it will wait
if it is used for only a moment in a rock's life
or for a thousand years in the tribal life, it will wait.

The workman has observed this waiting,
this slouched hanging from the board,
like the one square hanging in the ready
with a level to get it all straight

the way the other levels laid aside wait
with bubbles of air, like held breaths that can tell
when all is aligned and gravity agrees
that the work is plumb with the heart of the world.

Some say the patience of the workman
is the virtue of his shop, but, truly, the virtue
is motion. Rest is not how things get done.
Rest is how rust creeps into the world.

A WORKSHOP RUN BY RUST

Erosion is the mark of love
carved in chalky cliffs
and left to the wind to press
like an unrelenting kiss

that bruises and smothers
and smudges the names
from the hearts that were penknifed in stone,
stone having offered no heart of its own.

The workshop of rust works breathlessly
without compunction for the organic
shapings that work miracles from its slag,
and by their own devices make dirt

turn on rust and work
toward their own exhaustion
to keep the water at bay,
or make the breakwater dash

the crashing of the waves.
Rust shows no mercy;
it takes rust centuries
to bat an eye.

When the workman's reflection
catches on a chrome bend,
he senses an oblique adversary,
backwards working the shop to grist

for the other workshop where a pinch
sprinkled on the seasonal wheel
will run the natural migration of steel
and give a grape charge to ionise rust.

Then rust becomes food, turns flesh; angelic
engineer of all endings; keeper of the red gate;
whatever the finale's sound, says rust,
                        the end begins with a squeak.

THE APRON

A clean apron is a sign of illness.
Like a fresh-bristled broom,
a sharp pencil, an instrument
kept in tune, a stainfree apron

is suspect and should not be allowed
to leave the room unabused.
The workman's prized apron hangs alone
on a spike in a vertical beam

next to a clutch of aprons
that serve the craft
with varied cloths
for different moods of labour.

The favoured apron
is of leather, enwrought
with cracked, caked, baked-on grime
and eighty years of elbow grease.

It retains a paunchy curve or two
from one old man, who worked well enough
to keep it clean and pliable and non-flammable,
an armour against oil squirts and acid spills.

It rebuffed the meteoric showers tindered
by the friction of the circular saw
grinding through sheets of flashing; remained unaware
and undaunted by the glare of an occasional

slow comet of light shooting through the dim air.
The apron hasn't time enough to speculate
the hazards posed by the random arc
of a brief, minuscule spark.

The carbide teeth shrieked through wood,
the whirr and thump of the jackhammer drill
flicked shivers and sharp slivers at the chest.
The apron deflected them all with a tisk,

a sizzle, a kiss of smoke.
The apron carries scars enough
to keep a tribe of ears in wonder stories,
enough indeed for an odyssey:

at least one whole chapter devoted
to how the slumbering blowtorch roared
and spun to give the seasoned apron
that black-eyed burn and why.

Another chapter on the oblong patch
that covers the spot that fizzled away
when acid spilled its clawing biting frenzy
of bubbles over glove and apron,

invisible but for the foam at the mouth,
like some rabid spirit let loose in the shop,
what serendipitous sign spilled out that day,
and what it hissed.

Chapter upon chapter of soiling,
burn, and battle-scar
spanning generations of shop
in a sea of work in progress

for the home above the workshop,
the home the workshop serves,
maintains, and adorns with labour
and a labourer's rusty cicatrices,
    and a labourer's oily stains.

TOOL BOXES

More like crypts of plastic, or painted steel,
with smooth drawers and tiers that lift away
on rising hinges to reveal pick-up-sticks
in a bone-yard of drop-forged spanners tangled

in a jangle of allen keys and keys
that look like harmless, glinting lizards,
lockjaw pliers like a bunch of washed up silver fish
dried to steel by sun and sea-salt winds.

Every box is full to the brim; even
the portable cases are no longer for lugging,
too heavy, and filled all wrong for a single job,
but filled with still unheard-of tasks:

in a clatter of metal, in a clunk of clamps,
in a knock of wood, are worlds of work at rest;
at rest and fit for the palm of your hand
to raise a drawing-board dream.

HOW TO TREAT STEEL

There is a phase in the annealing
process, in which the steel
is so strenuously focused
on the proof of its own tensility,

that outwardly it appears cool,
but if a pair of tongs were to extend
an attentive hand, such a curious touch
would flinch from the heat;

and if to this touch were added
the incalculable weight that falls
from an affectionate gaze,
like motes in sunlight ever falling, never fallen,

but drifting like the pollen
from a tiger-lily picked in play,
if such lyrical abandon
were to well in one's eyes

and should light upon such steel,
it would split it from within
as if it were hit and jump apart
with a dull thud like axe-struck wood.

THE PEGBOARD

A heavy, mottled, antique funnel that's whirlpooled
at least a thousand liquids down sits
on the new pegboard with confident permanence;
a swiller of water and oil, acid and paint.

The saw hangs by its handle, its teeth
turned carefully inward because at its worst,
it will nick through the thick skin of the workman's hands
like a nail-toothed or staple-gunned board, lurking

in the woodwork, waiting to tear his fingertips,
till his hands, in anger, hammer them down.
He figures the pegboard will help master the mess:
when he needs something, habit will know where to find it.

He will waste no time thinking of anything other than
the task at hand. He reasons that true beauty
is the imagined made perfectly solid. But ultimately,
it is the mess that orders *him*, mars his constructions

with gouges and notches that freckle with birthmarks
places where a hand slipped or a tendon twanged,
and jarred the rhythms of making. Hours at a time,
upon the steady back of the workhorse, he's at it;

his tool-belt tossed aside, its contents scattered.
The pegboard behind him, a zodiac of power;
each tool, a constellation of duties that the workman
takes up for a season, forgets and sifts up again.

HAMMERS

The hammers swing their handles aslant,
and seem to sit like beakless woodpeckers,
the steel head fixed to the handle with an iron wedge,
a steel head like a crest flashing in the swing.

How different from hammer, though,
the hungry persistence of the bird at the bark
banging down into the homes that killed the tree;
their actions resemble, but their ends depart.

The tempered resilience of an inanimate head
taps out structures to an imagined plan
dreamed by a mind that is not on site
to say if the blueprint was interpreted right.

The drop-forged hammer-head with a handle of wood
absorbs the reverberating ricochet-force of metal-
pounding-metal; and when the workman throws
his sounds, he muscles more than his shoulders.

There is another, light-headed hammer
for when the finishing-work needs a delicate,
but fine decisive knock into a balsa-soft,
or pine-like spot that needs a nail to pin it.

And there's the mallet, of course, a small, wood
or rubber barrel for a bouncy head to strike more broadly
wood or steel without gouging half-moons
and crescent scars, leaving no heavenly sign

of the craftsman's heavy forearm
to trouble the work with its history,
to texture the product with its provenance
from scattered efforts and misfit pieces.

Signal
EDITIONS

Carmine Starnino, Editor
Michael Harris, Founding Editor

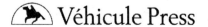 Véhicule Press